Anonymous

An appeal from the Protestant Association to the people of

Great Britain:

Concerning the probable tendency of the late Act of Parliament in favour

of the Papists

Anonymous

An appeal from the Protestant Association to the people of Great Britain:
Concerning the probable tendency of the late Act of Parliament in favour of the Papists

ISBN/EAN: 9783337730864

Printed in Europe, USA, Canada, Australia, Japan

Cover: Foto ©ninafisch / pixelio.de

More available books at **www.hansebooks.com**

AN

A P P E A L

FROM

THE PROTESTANT ASSOCIATION

TO

THE PEOPLE OF GREAT BRITAIN;

CONCERNING

THE PROBABLE TENDENCY OF THE LATE ACT OF PARLIAMENT IN FAVOUR OF THE PAPISTS.

To defign the Advancement of POPERY, is to defign the Ruin of the State, and the Deftruction of the Church; it is to facrifice the Nation to a double Slavery, to prepare Chains both for their Bodies and their Minds.   BP. SHERLOCK.

LONDON:

PRINTED BY J. W. PASHAM, BLACK-FRIARS;
AND SOLD BY J. DODSLEY, IN PALL-MALL; C. DILLY, IN
THE POULTRY; AND J. MATHEWS, IN THE STRAND.

MDCCLXXIX.

A N

APPEAL, &c. &c.

INTRODUCTION.

ALARMED at the indulgence granted to Papifts, by an Act lately paft in their favour, and well perfuaded that the principles of Popery deferve no fuch encouragement from any Proteftant ftate; we feel for ourfelves, we tremble for pofterity: and, having maturely deliberated on the confequences that moft probably will refult from this indulgence, we think it a duty we owe to religion and our country, to affociate; and, by every lawful method, to procure a remedy for the evils apprehended from its operation, and to preferve the ineftimable privileges, which, as Chriftians and members of fociety, we enjoy.

This Affociation is not formed to promote the views of party, or to embarrafs the meafures of government at this important crifis. It confifts of

B   Pro-

Proteftants, who will yield to none of their fellow-fubjects, in loyalty to His Majefty's perfon, or in zealous attachment to our happy conftitution.

If the doctrines held by Papifts were confined to matters of opinion in religion, and did not include political tenets of the moft dangerous tendency, they might expect the fame connivance, which has generally been extended to other erroneous fects: they might bow down to their images, fwallow the abfurd doctrine of tranfubftantiation, and amufe themfelves with dreams of Purgatory, without interruption: their ignorance and fuperftition would rather excite compaffion, than expofe them to the confequences of any Penal Statutes.

But, when Papifts thunder excommunication againft all who differ from them in opinion, and their religious profeffion itfelf breathes the very fpirit of perfecution and cruelty, againft thofe whom they anathematize as heretics; who, if Princes, are to be depofed and murdered; if fubjects, to be maffacred: when they avow fuch principles as thefe, what fecurity can be given to any ftate for their peaceable behaviour? and what claim can they have to toleration under any Proteftant government * ?

* See Archdeacon Blackburne's Confiderations on the prefent State of Popery.

It

It is not our defire to perfecute ; but, as Proteftants, we are concerned to fecure ourfelves and
pofterity from Popifh perfecution. When we call
to mind the Proteftant blood that has been fhed
by Papifts, both at home and in foreign countries,
we cannot but be excited to ufe every legal expedient, to prevent the return of fuch a national ca-
lamity.

Should the Papifts, in any future period, be
poffeffed of power, we have reafon to apprehend
that the fame principles would be productive of
the fame effects. Thefe principles they have never
publicly difavowed ; and, as Papifts, cannot, with
confiftency, difown : therefore, as they ftrike at
our liberties and lives, to tolerate perfons profeffing them, is to lay the axe to the root of our
deareft privileges and moft facred rights.

Impreffed with thefe confiderations, we would
now call the attention of our fellow-fubjects to
the following obfervations on *the late Act of Par-*
liament : and, if the matter contained in them be
true ; if our wifeft and beft laws againft Popery
be virtually repealed, and our conftitution actu-
ally endangered; what meafures fhould we adopt,
with what fpirit and unanimity fhould we act, to
preferve our civil and religious liberties from the
incroachments of Popery, and from its infeparable concomitant, ARBITRARY POWER ?

SECTION I.

Thoughts on Toleration, and how far it is consistent with our civil Constitution, and the preservation of the Protestant Religion, to extend it to the Papists.

IN order to gain a clearer idea of *Toleration*, let us inquire into the true nature of its opposite, which is *Persecution*.

Persecution consists in hurting a man in any of his natural or civil rights, without any crime committed on his part; but merely on account of the principles he holds, or the worship he performs; when those principles and that worship have nothing in them incompatible with the scriptures, the civil interests of the community, and the peace of the public; and though he be able and ready to give all legal security to the government for his peaceable behaviour.

Toleration is the very opposite of persecution, and, therefore, consists in the contrary spirit and conduct; that is, in allowing every man to profess his own faith, if not evidently repugnant to the holy scriptures, without the least injury done him in his civil rights, so long as he shall give proper security for his being a peaceable member of society.

Persecution, on the account of religion, is equally wicked and absurd, because it defeats its

own

own end; for, inftead of reconciling the mind to any fet of religious principles, it muft excite the utmoft horror and difguft; it may make hypocrites—it cannot make true converts.

The horrible effects of Perfecution by the Papifts in foreign countries, but more efpecially in our own, ought to touch the tendereft feelings of every true Proteftant. No language is fufficient to defcribe the injuftice and cruelty of fuch an infernal fpirit. To illuftrate the truth of thefe obfervations, let us, for a moment, turn our eyes to foreign countries; and what fcenes of cruelty have been acted under the aufpices of Popery! how many have been tortured on the rack, or cruelly murdered in the cells of the inquifition! how many have been dragged forth to difgrace, what is called, in thofe unhappy countries, an *auto da fé* *, but is rather an act of triumph over faith, humanity, and common fenfe. Is it not enough to condemn the innocent to flames, kindled by fuperftition, without leading them forth in mock proceffions, and cloathing them with *fan benitos*, or coats of devils, to expofe them to the infults of a barbarous multitude?—But why do we fpeak of cruelty to individuals only? Let us call to remembrance the maffacre at Paris, on the 24th of Auguft, 1572. There Popery appeared in its true colours, " drunken with the

* Act of Faith.

" blood

" blood of the faints, and with the blood of the
" martyrs of Jefus." Whilft Popery has exiftence upon earth, let it be remembered, though
to the difgrace of humanity; let it be remembered with horror, that on St. Bartholomew's-day,
thoufands and tens of thoufands of Proteftants were
murdered in France in cold blood; fuddenly
maffacred in their beds and houfes, by the cruelty and treachery of their Popifh fellow-fubjects,
at the very time they were careffed and courted;
and that this perfidious conduct met with the ap-
probation of his infallible holinefs, pope Gregory
XIIIth, of infamous memory, who went in folemn proceffion to St. Lewis's church, and infulted the goodnefs of the fupreme Being, by re-
turning thanks for the blood that had been fhed;
and, to preferve the remembrance of a tranfac-
tion fo meritorious, it was defcribed at Rome, in
a magnificent picture, intitled the TRIUMPH
of the CHURCH. Such is the faith that Papifts
keep with heretics; fuch the triumphs of the
church of Rome*.

But to come nearer home: in England, where
no inquifition was fuffered, Popery hath recorded
her name in characters of blood. During the
reign of queen Mary, how many of the moft
learned and pious men were brought to witnefs a
good confeffion at the ftake! The cruelty of Po-

* See Thuanus's Hiftory of France.

pifh

pifh perfecutors made no diftinction of age or fex, learned or unlearned, noble or ignoble: all fell alike the victims of their undifcerning bigotry. Nay, horrible to mention! pregnant women were burnt alive. And in the ifland of Guernfey, a fcene of almoft incredible barbarity was acted: " A mother and her two daughters being com- " mitted to the flames, one of them being mar- " ried, and in the laft month of her pregnancy, " was, by the violence of the pain, taken in la- " bour, and brought forth an infant; which a " humane bye-ftander refcued from the fire: " but after fome confultation, the magiftrate, " who fuperintended the execution, ordered the " innocent to be thrown back into the flames; " where it perifhed with the mother * ;" con- curring in opinion with Bellarmine, a cardinal of the firft note, who fays, " that if it were poffible " to root out heretics, without doubt they are to " be deftroyed *root* and *branch* †."

Smithfield, Oxford, Cambridge, moft of the public market-croffes, and many other places throughout the kingdom, have a voice crying aloud to Britifh Proteftants, BEWARE OF PO-PERY; and bear an unanimous and irrefragable teftimony, that Popery and Toleration never can agree ‡. O Britons! let not the blood of the

* See Smollet's Hiftory of England, vol. vi.
† See Bellarm, de laic.   ‡ See Fox's Martyrology.

martyrs

martyrs be forgotten, or their sufferings effaced from our memory, to the lateft pofterity.

From England, let us pafs to her fifter kingdom, Ireland; and behold more recent difplays of Popifh cruelty! Is the memorable and lamentable æra of 1641 fo foon forgotten? Are there none living, in thefe days, whofe anceftors fuffered by that unparalled maffacre, when the Papifts endeavoured to extirpate the Proteftants with fire, fword, and famine? Though the plot was difcovered, time enough to prevent the intended maffacre taking place in Dublin; yet, in the province of Ulfter, and other parts of the kingdom, near 100,000 Proteftants were butchered; with fuch circumftances of premeditated cruelty, as none but bigotted Papifts could have perpetrated. Such fpectacles of mifery and diftrefs muft have foftened any other hearts however favage or uncultivated. But Papifts not only infulted them in their fufferings, but triumphed in the hope, that the victims of their cruelty would be damned to all eternity *. The mind recoils from fuch fcenes of cruelty with horror; and, upon a review of all thefe melancholy facts, by what arguments from reafon, juftice, humanity, or piety, can the Toleration of fuch a religious

* See the Hiftory of England, and Sir John Parfon's Hiftory of this horrible maffacre.

profeffion

profeffion be defended in any free and Proteftant ftate?

It is alfo incompatible with the prefervation of our civil conftitution, to tolerate Popery; which not only enflaves the mind, but would bind nobles and people with the iron chains of defpotifm. It is a fyftem convenient for tyrants: we, at leaft of this country, have ever found it looking with a malignant afpect on freedom, and active in the retinue of Arbritary Power.

Popery abhors civil liberty, becaufe that is friendly to liberty of confcience: and it is a maxim of all Papifts, from which they never can, confiftently, depart, " that difobedience to the laws of the pope and church, not only excludes men from falvation; but is likewife a forfeiture of all civil rights and liberties whatfoever *."

Again,

* See No. 5, of Sir Richard Steel's Appendix to the Romifh Ecclefiaftical Hiftory, wherein are the following quotations:

" Heretics may lawfully be fpoiled of their goods, though " it be better to take them by authority."

" None are bound to reftore what they have been intrufted " with by heretics, or to perform any contract made with " them."

By pope Gregory the IXth's conftitutions, " A man, by " herefy, is deprived of all jurifdiction, whether natural, " civil, or politic."

" Heretics may not be termed either children or kindred; " but, according to the old law, thy hand fhall be upon them " to fpill their blood."

As

Again, do not the political principles of the Papifts oblige them to deny the fupremacy of the king of England ? Have they not, moreover, naturally fome obligations of intereft and attachment towards a *foreign claimant.* Did not James II. lofe his crown for adhering to Popery ?—Is Popery a crime in the eyes of Papifts ? Can they then ever look, on his lineal fucceffor, as only a

---

As a convincing proof of this, we give the following anecdote : " *John Diazius,* a *Spaniard,* became a Proteftant from reading the books of *Luther.* His brother *Alphonfus,* one of the pope's lawyers, hearing that his brother was turned Proteftant, came with all fpeed into *Germany,* bringing a notorious cut-throat with him, refolving either to bring him back to Popery, or to deftroy him.

When *Alphonfus* came to *Ratifbon,* his brother *John* was gone to *Newberg,* about the printing of *Bucer's* books, to which place *Alphonfus* followed him, and there they maintained many difputations upon religious matters ; but *Alphonfus* finding his brother fo ftedfaft in the belief of the truths of the gofpel, that neither the pope's agent, by his promifes or threats could terrify him, nor he by his perfuafions and pretenfions of brotherly love, could prevail upon him to return to Popery ; he feigned to take a moft friendly and affectionate leave of him, and departed ; but foon he returned with his ruffianly murderer, and by the way, they bought an hatchet of a carpenter. *Alphonfus* fent the ruffian in firft, difguifed, with letters to his brother, himfelf following behind ; and while *John Diazius* was reading the letters, this bloody murderer cleft his head with the hatchet, and taking horfe, they both rode away."

Biograph. Evangel. life of *Diazius.* A work now publifhing by the Rev. Mr. Middleton,

pretended

pretended prince ?—So that, whatfoever appearances they may affume, the ties of gratitude and affection bind their allegiance to the fucceffor of that Prince, who loft his crown in fupport of their caufe; and lead them to anathematize the Revolution, and reject the Act of Settlement, as an act of injuftice *.

---

* " It is not to be denied but that the pope, upon juft
" caufe, hath power to abfolve, both himfelf and all others,
" from the religious and legal obligation of an oath."

" After a prince is by name excommunicated by the pope,
" his fubjects are freed from their allegiance; his country
" becomes the right of catholics, who, beyond all contra-
" diction, exterminating the heretic inhabitants, may poffefs
" it as their own."

" The power of depriving kings of their crown, and em-
" perors of their dignities, for the good of the church and
" fouls, was always peculiar to the pope;

" Who hath no lefs authority, as Chrift's vicar, over Chrif-
" tians, than the fhepherd over his fheep."

" It is not lawful for Chriftians to tolerate any king, who
" draweth his fubjects into herefy."

" But fubjects ought to endeavour to fet up another in his
" place."

" They ought to expel him his kingdom, as the enemy of
" Chrift."

" This is the undoubted judgment of the moft learned, and
" agreeable to apoftolical truth."

" We, by our apoftolical authority, do abfolve all fub-
" jects from their oaths of fealty, which they have fworn to
" princes excommunicated.

" We excommunicate all heretic princes, and abfolve their
" fubjects from their oaths and duties of allegiance.

" *We*

That thefe were *formerly* the views of Papifts, is clearly evinced by their conduct in the rebellions of the year 1715 and 1745; that they are not *now*, we muft truft to the words and affurances of thofe men, whom no oaths can bind *.

With

" *We abfolve all fubjects of England from the oaths they have* " *taken to Elizabeth their queen.*"

See Richard Steel's Appendix.

* As Dr. Tucker, the Dean of Gloucefter, has taken upon him, in his late publication, entitled, " Thoughts on the Prefent State of Affairs," to affert, that the Papifts have been good fubjects for 100 Years paft, and that they had no hand in the rebellions of 1715 and 1745; we would beg leave to remind our readers, that 100 years have not yet elapfed fince the glorious Revolution ; and in how many plots they have been engaged againft the king, the government, and the Proteftant religion fince that happy event, none can be ignorant, but thofe who are unacquainted with the hiftory of Great Britain. As to their conduct in 1715, the following preamble of an Act of Parliament, made immediately after the fuppreffion of that unnatural rebellion, will be the fulleft confutation of the Rev. Dean's *panygeric* on the Papifts, and the beft evidence of the opinion our anceftors entertained of the principles of Popery, and of the *loyalty* of the Papifts on that occafion.——
" Whereas the Papifts within this kingdom, notwithftanding
" the tender regard that hath been fhewn them for many
" years laft paft, by omitting to put in execution the many Penal
" laws, which (on occafion of the many juft provocations they
" have given, and horrid defigns they have framed *for the de-*
" *ftruction of this kingdom, and the extirpation of the Proteftant*
" *religion)* have been made againft them ; and notwithftand-
" ing they have enjoyed, and do ftill enjoy, the protection and
" benefi

With refpect to the religious tenets of popery,
they are an offence to the very being and moral
perfections of God, irreconcileable to reafon, and
the

" benefit of the government, as well as the reft of his ma-
" jefty's fubjects, have, all, or the greateft part of them, been
" concerned in ftirring up and fupporting the late unnatural
" rebellion, for the dethroning and murdering his moft facred
" majefty ; for deftroying our prefent happy eftablifhment ; for
" fettling a Popifh pretender upon the throne of this kingdom ; for
" the deftruction of the Proteftant religion, and the cruel mur-
" dering and maffacreing its profeffors, by which they have
" brought a vaft expence upon this nation : And whereas it
" manifeftly appears by their behaviour, that they take upon
" themfelves to be obliged by the principles they profefs, to be ene-
" mies to His Majefty, and to the prefent happy eftablifhment, and
" watch for all opportunities of fomenting and ftirring up new
" rebellions and difturbances within the kingdom, and of INVIT-
" ING FOREIGNERS TO INVADE IT: And for as much as
" it is highly reafonable, that they fhould contribute a large
" fhare to all fuch extraordinary expences, as are or fhall be
" brought upon this kingdom by their treachery and inftiga-
" tion ; and to the end, that by paying largely to the late
" great expences by them brought upon this nation, they may
" be deterred, if poffible, from the like offences for the fu-
" ture, Geo. I. ftat. 2. c. 25."

It is alfo exprefsly mentioned in our ftatutes, that the defign " of the wicked, horrid, and unnatural rebellion in
" 1745, was to depofe and murder His moft facred Majefty, to
" fet up a POPISH PRETENDER, bred up and inftruct-
" ed in Romifh fuperftition and arbitrary principles on the
" throne, to the utter deftruction of the Proteftant religion, and
" the laws and liberties of this free conftitution :" from which
it

the moſt horrid corruption of divine revelation; and ought not to be tolerated, becauſe they impel the Papiſts, by a moſt intolerant ſpirit, to extirpate Proteſtants, under the name of *excommunicated heretics,*—becauſe it is one of their maxims, " that no faith is to be kept with heretics," by which the moſt ſacred ties of ſociety are diſſolved—becauſe they can have diſpenſations for perjury *, and paradiſe for murder and treaſon; and,

it evidently appears, that *ſo late* as the year 1745, Popery and Arbitrary Power were, in the judgment of our forefathers, inſeparably connected; and whether any, *but Papiſts*, would have attempted to depoſe and murder king George the IId, of glorious memory; to ſet up a Popiſh pretender, and utterly to deſtroy the Proteſtant religion, and the laws and liberties of this free conſtitution, (with the greateſt deference to the *bold aſſertion* of the Rev. Dean, in favour of the loyalty of Papiſts,) we appeal to the Proteſtants of Great Britain to determine.

* See the form of the oaths preſcribed by the late and former Acts of Parliament, which ſuppoſe that Papiſts, under the maſk of religion, are capable of the groſſeſt perjuries and moſt horrid treaſons; and alſo an extract in Sir Richard Steel's Appendix, from the oration of pope Sixtus the Vth, uttered in a conſiſtory at Rome, Sept. 2, 1759, wherein he commends, as wonderful and meritorious, the execrable murder committed by Jaques Clement, a Jacobine friar, on Henry III. king of France, and compares the conduct of the monk in perpetrating that execrable murder, with the conduct of Eleazar, and with that of Judith, in ſlaying Holofernes; and prefers the deed of the monk to both.

as pardons are to be bought on eafy terms, the
vileft crimes are committed without remorfe.

Upon the principles of common fenfe, what
can any man think of fuch contemptible doctrines, as the infallibility of a poor weak crea-
ture, and his fupremacy over all the empires and
kingdoms upon earth; yea, over all the worlds
of heaven, earth, and hell ?—What can any ra-
tional man think of a bit of bread being turned
into a human body and foul, and into the very
nature of God, or of worfhipping the fupreme
and omnipotent Being, under images of wood or
ftone, filver or gold ?—What can any virtuous
man think of this fupreme and infallible pope
felling pardons for all kinds of fins, and indul-
gences for all manner of wickednefs, for a thou-
fand years to come * ?—And, laftly, what can
any ferious man think of the damnable herefy of
for-

---

* From the following extracts of the fees of the Roman
chancery, taken from a book publifhed by the pope's authority, it appears that the prices of abfolution are as follow:

	l.	s.	d.
For lying with a woman in the church, and there committing other enormities	0	9	0
For grofs and wilful perjury —	0	9	0
For a layman for murdering a layman —	0	7	6
But for laying violent hands on a prieft, tho' without fhedding blood ———	0	10	6
For defiling a virgin ———	0	9	0
For a prieft or clergyman keeping a concubine	0	10	6

For

forbidding to marry, setting up the vain traditions of their church above the authority of the word of God; and of the Popish arrogance, in refusing the cup to the laity, and prohibiting millions of common people from reading the scriptures, though they have souls as infinite in value and duration, as the proudest prelates or highest monarchs upon earth?

To tolerate such opinions as these, is to insult the natural and moral perfections of that God, who gave us reason and immortality, and to encourage the practice of idolatry by law, in a Christian country. To tolerate Popery, is to be instrumental to the perdition of immortal souls now existing, and of millions of spirits, that at present have no existence, but in the prescience of God; and is the direct way to provoke the vengeance of an holy and jealous God, to bring down destruction on our fleets and armies, and ruin on ourselves and our posterity.

- For committing incest	———	0 7	6
But, for forging the Pope's hand-writing		1 7	7

See No. 2, of the Appendix to the aforesaid history of Sir Richard Steel.

SECTION

SECTION. II.

*A View of the principal Laws that were in Force
against the Papists before they were altered by the
late Act of Parliament; and of the Spirit in
which they were executed.*

TO know how far a mitigation of the Penal
laws against the Papists was expedient or
neceffary, a view of the laws fhould be taken,
and likewife of the mild fpirit, in which they
were enforced.

To enter into a minute detail of the numerous
Acts in our books against Popery, would be te-
dious, and exceed the limits of our prefent
publication : it will be fufficient, therefore, to
felect a few of the feveral ftatutes on this fubject : amongst which, the principal laws against
JESUITS AND POPISH PRIESTS—HEARING AND SAY-
ING MASS—POPISH BOOKS AND RELICS—PAPISTS
KEEPING SCHOOLS—AND PURCHASING AND IN-
HERITING ESTATES, demand our more immediate
attention.

By the 27th of Eliz. c. 2. no jefuit or Popifh
prieft fhall come into, or be in the realm, on pain
of high treafon, unlefs he conform ; and any perfon knowingly receiving, or relieving fuch, is
guilty of felony, without benefit of clergy.

By

By divers fubfequent ftatutes of Eliz. and Jam. feveral other penalties are inflicted ; and it is particularly enacted by the ftatute of 3d Jam. c. 4. that if any perfon fhall put in practice to reconcile any fubjects to Popery, or, if any perfon fhall be willingly fo reconciled, he, his aiders, and maintainers, fhall be guilty of high treafon.

By the 11th and 12th of Wm. IIId. c. 4. any perfon apprehending any Popifh bifhop, prieft, or jefuit, and profecuting him, till he was convicted of exercifing any part of his ecclefiaftical function, *was* (for this is now repealed) entitled to the reward of 100l. and any Popifh bifhop, prieft, or jefuit, fo exercifing his function, (except in foreign minifters houfes) *was* adjudged to perpetual imprifonment.

By the 23d Eliz. c. 1. and feveral fubfequent ftatutes, perfons hearing or faying mafs were liable to forfeitures and imprifonment ; and by the above ftatute of Wm. IIId. any Popifh bifhop, prieft, or jefuit, that fhould fay mafs, (except in foreign minifters houfes) *was* adjudged to perpetual imprifonment.

By feveral ftatutes of Edward VIth. Eliz. and Jam. Ift. perfons having in cuftody, bringing from beyond the feas, printing, felling, buying, or receiving any Popifh books or relics, are made liable to pecuniary penalties ; and, in fome cafes, to imprifonment, and the pain of incurring a premu-

premunire ; and the books and relics are to be burned, and defaced, and magiftrates are thereby impowered to fearch for the fame.

There are many ftatutes in our books againft fending children to be educated in Popifh prin-ciples ; and by the ftatutes of 13th and 14th Car. IId. c. 4. and 17th Car. IId. c. 2. all perfons (and Papifts amongft others) are prohibited from teach-ing fchool, upon pain of fine and imprifonment ; unlefs they be licenfed by the ordinary, and con-form to the liturgy of ihe eftablifhed church * ; and by the 11th and 12th Wm. IIId. any Papift keeping fchool, or taking upon him the govern-ment or boarding of youth, *was* adjudged to per-petual imprifonment.

The only ftatute that incapacitated Papifts from purchafing or inheriting eftates, was the above-mentioned Act of Wm. IIId. by which they were difabled to purchafe, and rendered in-capable of inheriting, or taking any lands by de-fcent, devife, or limitation ; but the fame were given to the next of kin, being Proteftants.

Thus ftood the principal laws againft Popery before the late Act of Parliamant was paffed. Laws that, from time to time, were rendered ne-ceffary, by the turbulent conduct of the Papifts:

---

* By an Act paffed in the laft feffion, Proteftant Diffen-ters taking the oath therein mentioned, are qualified to teach and keep fchools.

　　　　　　　　every

every additional feverity being occafioned by the difcovery of frefh infurrections againft government; which will appear very evident to thofe, who confult the hiftory of the time wherein thefe ftatutes were enacted *.

Perhaps it may appear ftrange, in this day, that the Papifts were, by fo many ftatutes, made fubject to the penalties of high treafon: but this difficulty vanifhes, when we confider that our anceftors knew, by dear bought experience, that the principles of Papifts neceffarily lead to treafonable practices againft the ftate; fince they own implicit obedience to a foreign head, who claims a power of abfolving fubjects from their allegiance, and depofing and excommunicating princes for herefy.

To this fource we muft afcribe the many nefarious attempts that they have made on our excellent Conftitution, and on the perfons of our Sovereigns fince the Reformation: and from this fource we muft expect ruin to ourfelves and pofterity, whenever thofe, who have always had the will, fhall have the power, to deftroy us.

Should the laws, as they thus ftood againft the Papifts, appear too fevere; let it be remembered, as a judicious writer obferves, " that they

* See Bifhop Gibfon's Fifth Paftoral Letter, entitled, " The Danger and Mifchiefs of Popery." Sec. 6 and 7.

" who

" who made thefe laws, had an opportunity of
" contemplating the naked features of Popery,
" ftripped of all difguife." They faw the bitter
enmity it bore to the civil and religious rights
of mankind; and were, confequently, better
judges of what was neceffary for the future fecurity of the Britifh conftitution, than we of this
generation, who (thanks to a kind Providence)
have had no fuch experience *.

Had the promoters of the late repealing ftatute looked back, and placed themfelves in the
fituation of our anceftors; had they taken
a retrofpective view of maffacres in cold blood,
of flames fcarce extinguifhed, of plots and rebellions with difficulty difcovered and fuppreffed;
they would have been alarmed at the malignant
afpect of Popery, and *fuch an Act* would never
have paffed fo unanimoufly through the Britifh
fenate.

Having thus briefly examined the laws as they
formerly ftood, let us now confider the fpirit in
which they were executed; a fpirit of lenity and
moderation. They were feldom enforced, but
when the rebellious conduct of the Papifts rendered it abfolutely neceffary, and brought down
the vengeance of Penal ftatutes on their heads:

* See Archdeacon Blackburn on 'The prefent State of Popery, page 26.

and even then, they were inflicted by the hand of difcriminating juftice; not confounding the innocent with the guilty.

Notwithftanding all that we are told of the feverity of thefe ftatutes, they are mild, when compared with the bloody edicts now in full force againft Proteftants in Popifh countries. Whilft Papifts in England are claiming Toleration, Proteftants in France are expofed to perfecution, by the repeal of the edict of Nantz: and in other Popifh countries, Proteftants are, by law, condemned to death.—Aftonifhing contraft! that needs only to be c nfidered, to evidence the impropriety of the late repeal.

The wifdom and policy of the laws againft Popery have been proved by the experience of above two hundred years; and it is to them we are at this day indebted, under divine Providence, for the prefervation of our rights and liberties, and for the fettlement of the crown in the illuftrious houfe of Hanover.

If we may believe the very advocates for tolerating Popery, by thefe laws Papifts were difcouraged, their numbers in England confiderably decreafed, and Papifts themfelves conftrained to become good fubjects: and ought laws, whofe wholefome feverity hath produced fuch falutary effects, to have been effentially changed, or virtually repealed?

Befides,

Befides, was there any application from the Papifts, complaining to government of the rigorous execution of thofe laws, that occafioned the late alteration to be made therein ? It is not pretended that there was : the Papifts would not venture fuch an affertion ; nor could it have gained credit, if they had. How far the laws themfelves are materially affected by the late Act of Parliament, will appear from a perufal of the next fection.

SECTION III.

Confiderations on the late Act of Parliament ; and the Alterations made thereby in the Penal laws againft the Papifts.

THE Act of William IIId. which was the object of the late repeal, was, with great propriety, entitled, " An Act for the further preventing of the growth of Popery." The preamble recites, " That there had been of late a much greater refort into this kingdom than formerly of Popifh bifhops, priefts, and jefuits, and that they did very openly, and in an infolent manner, affront the laws, and daily endeavour to pervert His Majefty's natural born fubjects; which had been occafioned by neglect of the due execution of the laws already in force." For preventing

C 4   the

the further growth of Popery, and of such treasonable and execrable designs against His Majesty's person and government, and the established religion, as had lately, as well as frequently theretofore, been brought to light, and happily defeated, by the wonderful Providence of God; it was thereby enacted, amongst other things, "That any persons, who should apprehend any Popish bishop, priest, or jesuit, and prosecute them, till they were convicted of saying mass, or exercising any part of their office or function, should be entitled to 100l. reward; and any such bishops, priests, or jesuits, so convicted, or any other Papists that should keep school, or take upon them the education or government of youth, were adjudged to perpetual imprisonment: and Papists, not taking the oaths of allegiance and supremacy, within the time therein limited, were disabled, and made incapable of inheriting, or purchasing lands; which were given to the next of kin, being a Protestant."

Whatever severity may appear in the penalties, it is evident, from the very words of the preamble, that they were warranted by the insolent conduct and treasonable practices of the Papists. And ought such wholesome provisions to have been repealed; unless there be sufficient reason to apprehend that Popish bishops, priests, and jesuits will not now resort hither, in as great numbers

bers as they did at that time, to repeat their pernicious practices; especially jesuits, who are *now*,
what they were not *then*, the *outcasts* even of
Popish countries?

There are but few instances, wherein this Act
hath been enforced: the heavy penalty of perpetual imprisonment intimidated the jesuits of
that day, who crossed the seas in shoals, and rendered the execution of it almost unnecessary.
The clauses relating to estates, were a stab to the
vitals of Popery; which, being deprived of the
means of acquiring landed influence, was discou-
raged, and gradually declined.

But, by the preamble of an Act made in the
18th Geo. IIId. entitled, "An Act for relieving
His Majesty's subjects, professing the Popish religion, from certain penalties and disabilities im-
posed on them by the above-mentioned Act of
Wm. IIId." we are told, That it is expedient to
repeal the very provisions, which had been productive of such happy effects.

And, accordingly, it is thereby enacted, "That
so much of the said Act as relates to the apprehending, taking, or prosecuting, of Popish bishops,
priests, or jesuits; and also, so much of the said
Act, as subjects Popish bishops, priests, or jesuits,
and Papists, or persons professing the Popish religion, and keeping school, or taking upon themselves the education or government of youth,
within

within thefe realms of England, or the dominions thereto belonging, to perpetual imprifonment; and alfo, fo much of the faid Act as dif-
ables perfons educated in the Popifh religion, or
profefling the fame, under the circumftances
therein mentioned, from inheriting or purchafing
any manors, lands, tenements, or hereditaments; and gives to the next of kin, being a Proteftant, a right to have and enjoy fuch manors;
lands, tenements, hereditaments, fhall be, and the
fame, and every claufe, matter, and thing therein before-mentioned, is, and are, thereby repealed,
for the relief of all Papifts who fhall, within the
time therein-mentioned, take the following oath :"

" I A. B. do fincerely promife and fwear, That
" I will be faithful and bear true allegiance to
" His Majefty king George the Third, and him
" will defend, to the utmoft of my power, againft
" all confpiracies and attempts whatever that fhall
" be made againft his perfon, crown, or dignity;
" and I will do my utmoft endeavour to difclofe
" and make known to His Majefty, his heirs, and
" fucceffors, all treafons and traiterous confpira-
" cies which may be formed againft him or them;
" and I do faithfully promife to maintain, fup-
" port, and defend, to the utmoft of my power,
" the fucceffion of the crown in His Majefty's fa-
" mily, againft any perfon or perfons whatfoever;
" hereby

" hereby utterly renouncing. and abjuring any
", obedience or allegiance unto the.perſon taking
" upon himſelf the ſtile and title .of prince of
" Wales, in the lifetime of his father, and who,
" ſince his death, is ſaid to have aſſumed the ſtile
" and title of king of Great Britain, by the name
" of Charles the Third, *and to any* other perſon
" claiming or pretending a right to the crown of
" theſe realms ; and I do ſwear, that I do reject
" and deteſt, as an unchriſtian and impious poſi-
" tion, That it is lawful to murder or deſtroy any
" perſon or perſons whatſoever, for or under pre-
" tence of their being heretics ; and alſo that un-
" chriſtian and impious principle, that no faith is
" to be kept with heretics : I further declare,
" that it is no article of my faith, and that I do
" renounce, reject, and abjure, the opinion, that
" princes excommunicated by the pope and coun-
" cil, or by any authority of the ſee of Rome, or
" by any authority whatſoever, may be depoſed
" or murdered by their ſubjects, or any perſon
" whatſoever : and I do declare, that I do not be-
" lieve that the pope of Rome, or any other fo-
" reign prince, prelate, ſtate, or potentate, hath,
" or ought to have, any *temporal* or *civil juriſ-*
" *diction*, power, ſuperiority, or pre-eminence, di-
" rectly or indirectly, within this realm. And I do
" ſolemnly, in the preſence of God, profeſs, teſ-
" tify, and declare, that I do make this declara-
" tion, and every part thereof, in the plain and or-

" dinary

" dinary fenfe of the words of this oath ; without
" any evafion, equivocation, or mental referva-
" tion whatever; and without any difpenfation al-
" ready granted by the pope, or any authority of
" the fee of Rome, or any perfon whatever ; and
" without thinking that I am or can be acquitted
" before God or man, or abfolved of this decla-
" ration, or any part thereof, although the pope,
" or any other perfons or authority whatfoever,
" fhall difpenfe with or annul the fame, or de-
" clare that it was null or void."

It is evident, therefore, that, by the Act of
Geo. IIId. the moft material parts of the ftatute
of Wm. IIId. exprefsly enacted *for the further
preventing the growth of Popery*, are actually repealed: and though it be faid, that thefe are only
detached parts of a fingle Act of Parliament; yet
it will appear, from the following confiderations,
that the laws, which, we are told, now remain in
force againft the Papifts, are become a body without a foul; there is no fpirit remaining to enforce
them, nor any encouragement to put them into
execution.

By the repeal of the laft and moft fpirited Act
againft Popifh bifhops, priefts, jefuits, and fchool-
mafters, are not all former ftatutes virtually repealed or invalidated? To rake into the embers
of thofe antient laws, would appear malicious, in
the judgment of our modern law-givers: nor
could

could it be expected that such profecutions would be countenanced, in any court of juftice; when the very foundation, on which they formerly ftood, is removed by the Act of Geo. IIId.

What wife ends can it anfwer, to enforce the antique ftatutes for deftroying and defacing Popifh books and relics, (which may be deemed innocent in their operation, when compared with the fubtilty of thofe, by whom they were promulgated and difperfed) fince Popifh bifhops, priefts, jefuits, and fchool-mafters, may now teach and propagate their erroneous principles, in their own perfons, to the feduction of the rifing generation?

To repeal an Act to prevent the refort of Popifh bifhops, priefts, and jefuits to thefe realms, is a ftrong encouragement, not to fay, invitation, to them to come over in abundance. If it be objected, that there are two ftatutes ftill in force, one of Eliz. and another of Jam. declaring fuch offenders to be guilty of high-treafon; it is obvious to anfwer, that the fubfequent law, which condemned thefe offenders to perpetual imprifonment, and the laft Act which has revoked that fentence, on condition of taking the oaths, have virtually repealed the two preceding ftatutes. For what the law declares not to be deferving of banifhment, cannot be judged worthy of death. Our legiftature, con-

fequently

fequently, in effect, has declared, that, as there is now no law in force againft propagating Popifh errors, every one who engages in the pernicious office, may proceed in it without danger or fear of moleftation.

By the laft fection of this repealing ftatute, it is provided, " That nothing in that Act fhould " be conftrued to extend to any Popifh bifhop, " prieft, jefuit, or fchoolmafter, who fhall not " have taken, or fubfcribed the oath, before a " profecution fhall have been commenced againft " him :" which plainly implies, that it was expected by the Legiflature, that Popifh bifhops, priefts, jefuits, and fchoolmafters, would now refort hither; and is a tacit licence for them to exercife the duties of their function, upon condition of taking the oath therein prefcribed.

If it were not meant, that all who qualified, by taking the oath required to be taken by the late ftatute, fhould be thereby fcreened from the penalties of all former Acts; why was that provifion inferted, to make a favourable diftinction between thofe who have taken the oath before they fhall have been profecuted, and thofe who have not? whilft thofe who refufed or neglected to conform, were liable to a penalty of perpetual imprifonment; others, who fubmitted to the terms of the Legiflature, would be in a

much

much worfe fituation. The Popifh bifhops, jefuits, and clergy would think themfelves little obliged to our fenators, to fave them from a prifon, whilt they left them expofed to a gibbet; and, after all their conformity, if the old laws be not underftood to be virtually repealed, be liable to an arraignment for high treafon, and fubject to an ignominous death.

If the laws againft priefts and jefuits be virtually repealed, it neceffarily follows that the laws againft Popifh chapels, and hearing and faying mafs, are in the fame fituation. It would be in vain to relieve the former from the penalties of coming to, or being found within, thefe realms, if by fhutting up and prohibiting the latter, they are prevented from exercifing their ecclefiaftical function; as they are too affiduous to be idle in *fuch a caufe*, and have no bufinefs in this country, but to pervert the ignorant and unwary.

The only ftatutes, in which the Papifts are, *by name*, prohibited from keeping fchools, is now repealed. They were indeed, amongft other perfons, prohibited from keeping fchools, by the Acts of 13th and 14th Car. IId. c. 4 and 17th Car. IId. c. 2. unlefs they we relicenfed by the ordinary, and fubfcribed a declaration of conformity to the eftablifhed church: but it is well known how little thefe ftatutes have been regarded

garded of late years; and, as Papiſts are now no longer awed by the penalty of that clauſe in the ſtatute of Wm. IIId. many Popiſh ſchools and ſeminaries of learning will, doubtleſs, be added to thoſe already opened, throughout the kingdom.

The ſtatute of Wm. IIId. was enacted to prohibit their teaching, becauſe it had been found, by experience, that the former laws were inſufficient for that purpoſe ; but that is one of the detached parts of the laws againſt Popery, which is totally altered by the Act lately paſſed for their relief. It is in vain to enforce the obſolete laws to prevent the ſending of our children to foreign ſeminaries, to be inſtructed in " *the rankeſt principles of ſedition and rebellion* ;" when they may now be taught at home, without the riſque of croſſing the ſeas, and at the eaſieſt expence to their parents *.

Nor can we blame the Papiſts, for conſtruing all former ſtatutes on the ſubject as virtually re-repealed, when the *only* clauſe, in which they are *expreſsly named*, is no longer in force. They have reaſon to think themſelves licenſed to teach, as well as preach ; and we have too many recent inſtances to prove by their conduct, that theſe are their ſentiments. How fatal the conſequences to poſterity !

* See Biſhop Gibſon's 5th Paſtoral Letter, page 26.

Our

Our anceftors well knew that landed property and parliamentary influence were infeparable; and, therefore, to form a bulwark for the defence of our conftitution, wifely concluded, that it was their indifpenfible duty, not only by the Teft Act to exclude Papifts from fitting in the houfe; but to prevent them from interfering in the choice of reprefentatives, by depriving them of the means of influence amongft the electors.

· For thefe important ends, by the abovementioned Act of Wm. IIId. Papifts were difabled to purchafe, and incapacitated to inherit, any landed property; and their eftates were given to the next of kin, being Proteftants. By thefe means Proteftantifm was encouraged, the wings of Popifh arrogance were clipped, and they, being no longer in a fituation to acquire landed property, loft their influence; and our liberties have been preferved to this day.

The feverity of this ftatute was felt in its operation by Papifts of the laft century; and government has experienced the policy of it, from its effects, in this. Papifts, incapacitated to purchafe lands, were neceffitated to lay out their monies in the funds, to contribute to the fupport of the ftate; and the Papifts, in our day, have fcarcely felt any inconvenience therefrom; having been habituated, for fo many

D   years,

years, to acquire a monied intereft, in lieu of landed property. But this barrier is now removed; thefe claufes are all repealed; and Papifts are enabled to purchafe what they can, and capacitated to inherit all they purchafe.

If we attend to the form of the oath to be now taken by the Papifts in the laft Act of Parliament, we fhall perceive a very ftriking variation between that and the oath of Supremacy of Geo. 1ft. ftat. 2. c. 13; by that, every Proteftant, and all other perfons are required, on their oath, to declare, that no foreign prince, perfon, prelate, ftate, or potentate *hath, or ought to have,* any jurifdiction, power, fuperiority, preeminence, or authority, " *ecclefiaftical* or *fpiri-* " *tual,*" within thefe realms. But in the laft ftatute, *to accommodate the Papifts,* and to avoid incroaching on their obedience and fubmiffion to their Spiritual Father, the words, " *ecclefiaftical* " or *fpiritual,*" are omitted, and the words, " *temporal* or *civil,*" fubftituted; by which it is plainly declared, that the Legiflature, confcious of the jurifdiction of the pope over every Papift within this realm, and that the Papifts, as fuch, could never confcientioufly abjure the fame; have *defignedly* changed thofe material words, and thereby recognized, within thefe realms, *the ecclefiaftical and fpiritual jurifdiction of the pope,* and all that are in authority under him.

And

And notwithſtanding the oath is guarded, as much as it is poſſible for any form of words to guard againſt mental reſervations and jeſuitical evaſions; yet, it is evident, that, as the Papiſts hold the principles aſcribed to them in the oath, (and if not, why aſcribe them?) they may, with the greateſt deliberation, commit perjury; and, without inconſiſtency, abjure their faith, ſince their conduct would be held meritorious in a Romiſh conſiſtory; and they would be intitled, not only to diſpenſations, but to commendations, for ſo doing.

But ſuppoſing, which cannot be admitted, that Papiſts take the oath in ſincerity, and ſwear without any mental reſervation; how few, in proportion to the number of the Papiſts, will be under the neceſſity of appearing to take the oath? biſhops, prieſts, jeſuits, ſchoolmaſters, and thoſe who are deſirous to capacitate themſelves to purchaſe or inherit eſtates, muſt ſubmit to the terms preſcribed; but how few are they, when compared with the bulk of the Papiſts in this nation? and it is unreaſonable to ſuppoſe that any amongſt them will take this oath, except with views to their ſecurity or intereſt.

Conſidering the inattentive manner in which oaths of this nature are adminiſtered in our public courts, it will be a fortunate circumſtance for

the

the more fcrupulous amongft the Papifts, who, taking the advantage of the hurry and confufion which generally attends this kind of bufinefs, may repeat after the officer as much as they pleafe, and omit the reft ; and yet, upon taking *fuch* an oath, in *fuch* a manner, Papifts are to be intitled to relief under that Act of Parliament.

Is it not evident from the foregoing obferva-tions, that all the laws againft Popery are virtual-ly, and the moft effential and important, actu-ally repealed ? and that, though the late ftatute be not entitled, *An Act for the toleration of Pope-ry* within his Majefty's dominions ; yet Papifts, conforming to the terms thereof, have a right to expect *at leaft* a connivance on the part of the Le-giflature, which will be equivalent thereto in every refpect.

A learned commentator on the laws of Eng-land, has obferved, that " if a time fhould ever " arrive, when all fears of a pretender fhall have " vanifhed, and the power and influence of the " pope fhall become feeble, ridiculous, and def- " picable, not only in England, but in every " kingdom of Europe ; it probably would not " then be amifs, to review and foften thefe rigo- " rous edicts ; at leaft, till the *civil principles* of " the Roman Catholics called *again* upon the le- " giflature to renew them." But there is no rea-

I

fon to conclude that this is the time: the influence of the pope is not yet become ridiculous and defpicable in foreign countries; and Papifts in England pay the moft implicit obedience to every mandate of the Roman fee.

But if fuch a period fhould arrive, might not a line be drawn between *foftening* and *repealing?* It would be a dangerous experiment to wait till the civil principles of Papifts again expofed them to the difpleafure of the law. We have reafon to believe that, whatever their civil principles might be, their conduct would involve them in fecrecy; nor would they venture to ftrike a blow, that might difcover them, till they had undermined our conftitution and effected our deftruction; and then it would be too late for the wifdom of the Legiflature to interfere.

Therefore, from all thefe confiderations, may we not conclude, that the late indulgence is impolitic and inexpedient; and that this is not the time to repeal the ftatutes againft Popery?

SECT.

SECTION IV.

Obfervations on the manner, in which the late Act was obtained; on the principal Arguments in its Favour; and on the fatal Confequences, which will moft probably refult from it.

WHEN we confider how far the whole fyftem of the law againft Popery is affected by the late Act of Parliament, it is reafonable to fuppofe, that an Act of fuch national importance would have been introduced in the moft public ma ner. Ought not an alarm to have been founded throughout the kingdom, that the fenfe of the people might have been known, before laws, in which they were fo effentially concerned, were fo materially altered; and before the ftructure, which the wifdom of our anceftors was fo many years employed in raifing againft the dangerous encroachments of Popery, was to be demolifhed at one blow.

Inftead of which, without any previous notice, the Act was introduced, in the moft private manner—at the end of a feffion—to a thin houfe: many of the members having retired to their country feats; it being underftood that the principal bufinefs was finifhed, and that no new matter of an interefting nature, would be taken up at that advanced feafon of the year. Thofe who were zealous for its fuccefs, might be confcious, that,

if

if there had been time for reflecting on the Act and its confequences, it never would have paffed: it was, therefore, hurried through the houfe, without a review of the ftatutes, as they then ftood; or a mature confideration, how far they would be altered by the paffing of this Popifh Bill.

The fituation of thofe at the helm was delicate: it was dangerous, at fuch a crifis, to provoke the refentment of a numerous body of Papifts, by oppofing the bill; they were ignorant of the fentiments of the people; and, being thus furprifed, thought it politic to acquiefce. The bifhops had not time fufficiently to deliberate on it; and were tender of appearing enemies to Toleration. Thus the mifchief was done, before the defign was made known; and, confequently, before it could be prevented.

There *has been* a time, when the fpirit of the people would, and juftly too, have been *roufed* at fuch furreptitious conduct; but, alas, for the welfare of thefe realms! a fpirit of fupinenefs and indifference, as to the interefts of religion and liberty, ftrangely pervades the kingdom; and the zeal of our anceftors, either for the Proteftant caufe, or for our glorious Conftitution, is no where to be found *.

But

* In a tract publifhed in 1753, printed for Dodfley, in Pall-Mall, intitled, " A brief Account of the Vandois, his

" Sardinian

But this Act had a different fate in Scotland: it was not paſſed in that ſeſſion; therefore the people had full time to foreſee its fatal effects, and to prevent their taking place. And though we cannot approve the conduct of the mobs at Edinburgh and Glaſgow; yet the ſpirited and ſuccefsful oppoſition in Scotland to the Popiſh bill, will, for ever, endear thoſe who were con-cerned in it, to every true Proteſtant.

The principal arguments in favour of the Bill, are the following,—that Papiſts are become good ſubjects, and therefore ought no longer to be ex-poſed to the penalties of ſuch ſevere ſtatutes;—that, in the preſent ſituation of affairs, the late repealing Act was neceſſary, to conciliate their affection to government—and that no bad conſe-quences can reſult therefrom, as Popery is not now of an intolerant and perſecuting ſpirit.

" Sardinian Majeſty's Proteſtant Subjects in the vallies of Pi-
" edmont, &c." there is a remarkable inſtance of the zeal of
Engliſhmen for the Proteſtant religion.' When theſe inof-
fenſive people were perſecuted and impoveriſhed by Popiſh
cruelty, " the Dutch, the Swifs, and the Germans (ſaith
" the author) had relieved the Vandois by benefactions: but
" perhaps there is no inſtance in hiſtory of any nation inter-
" poſing ſo warmly for another, as the Engliſh did, at this
" time, for a poor people, removed from them at an im-
" menſe diſtance; in an inland country, and connected by
" no reaſons of policy or intereſt." And we are informed in
the margin, that the collections in England amounted to
38097 l. 7 s. 3 d. a noble inſtance of laudable zeal, worthy
of imitation in the preſent day!

If

If the Papifts were rendered firm in their allegiance, by the operation of the wife enactions, which are now repealed; why were they repealed? We have lately had little opportunity of proving their fincerity: for the enemies of the Proteftant fucceffion were fo effectually crufhed during the rebellions in 1715 and 1745; that, whatever their inclinations might have been, they could have no profpect of fuccefs, in any plots, without imminent danger to themfelves.

Whatever the exigencies of government might require; that a *Proteftant ftate* fhould be indebted to the *arms of Papifts* for its fupport, is a circumftance truly alarming, and worthy the moft ferious confideration of every Briton.

In the beginning of the late war, our affairs affumed a gloomy afpect: but did we arm the Papifts for our defence? Were we indebted to them for the glorious victories of 1759? Was it not the wifdom of our anceftors, to diftruft the proferffions, and difarm the profeffors of Popery? And fhould we put fwords into the hands of Papifts, God only knows how foon they might be turned againft our own lives, and be employed in fubverting our moft valuable interefts *.

As to the perfecuting fpirit of Popery; it is to this day, and ever will be, the fame: it cannot be otherwife, whilft they maintain its two fun-

* See Bifhop Ufher's Proteftation againft Popery.

damental

damental tenets, PAPAL SUPREMACY and INFALLIBILITY: the apparent difference muſt be aſcribed to their want of power *.

By rejecting their idolatrous ſuperſtition and vain traditions, we are become heretics and ſchiſmatics, in the judgment of the ſee of Rome: and doth not the pope yearly excommunicate us as ſuch, denounce the moſt awful curſes againſt us, and declare our deſtruction to be a meritorious work? That all this is not mere form and ceremony, but a direction zealouſly purſued, whenever it is practicable; is evident from the bloody inquiſition, and the conduct of Papiſts in all kingdoms, where Popery is unreſtrained by law †.

Popery

* "Can it be worth while (ſays the learned and ingenious Biſhop Hurd) to ſpend words in fixing this charge of *intolerance* on the church of Rome, when her ableſt advocates, even in our days, openly triumph in it." For proof of this, he refers to *Mr. Crevier's hiſtory de l' Univerſite' de Paris* tom. iii. *l. vi. page* 435. *Paris,* 1761. Where that eminent writer very roundly defends the *murder* of the Bohemian Martyrs at Conſtance, and the *fraud and ill faith,* through which the *pious and tender hearted fathers* of that council ruſhed to the perpetration of it. See Introduction to the Study of the Prophecies, 2d. edit. p. 382.

† The following extracts, from the form of Excommunication pronounced at *Rome* on *Maunday-Thurſday,* demonſtrate the *benign* ſpirit by which the Papiſts are actuated towards thoſe whom they deem hereticks.

The

Popery has long been chained in Britain: the confequences of unchaining it will be dreadful
to

The Title runs thus : " *The Excommunication and Anathematization of all Hereticks whatfoever, and their favourers, and Schifmaticks, or of thofe who violate the Ecclefiaftical Liberty, or any ways infringe the contents of this Bull, which is wont to be publifhed on* Maunday-Thurfday.

" Sect. 1. We excommunicate and anathematize in the name of God Almighty, Father, Son and Holy Ghoft, and by the authority of the bleffed apoftles Peter and Paul, and by our own, all Huffites, Wickliphifts, Lutherans, Zuinglians, Calvinifts, Hugonots, Anabaptifts, Trinitarians, and Apoftates from the Chriftian faith, and all other hereticks by whatfoever name they are called, and of whatfoever fect they be : as alfo their adherents, receivers, favourers, and generally any defenders of them ; together with all who without our authority, or that of the apoftolick fee, knowingly read, keep, print, or any ways for any caufe whatfoever publickly or privately on any pretext or colour, defend their books containing herefy, or treating of religion ; as alfo fchifmaticks, and thofe who withdraw themfelves, or recede obftinately from the obedience of us, or the bifhop of *Rome* for the time being."

" Sect. 2. Further, we excommunicate and anathematize all and fingular, of whatfoever ftation, degree or condition they be ; and interdict all univerfities, colleges and chapters, by whatfoever name they are called ; who appeal from the orders or decrees of us, or the popes of *Rome* for the time being to a future general council ; and thofe by whofe aid and favour the appeal was made."

" Sect. 16. Alfo thofe who upon this account directly or indirectly hinder archbifhops, bifhops, and other fuperior and inferior prelates, and all other ordinary ecclefiaftical judges whatfoever by any means, either by imprifoning or mo-
lefting

to posterity, as the principles of Popery are still the same. Popes and general councils are still infallible :

letting their agents, proctors, domesticks, kindred on both sides, or by any other way from exerting their ecclesiastical jurisdiction against any persons whatsoever, according as the canons and sacred ecclesiastical constitutions and decrees of general councils, and especially that of *Trent*, do appoint; as also those who after the sentence and decrees of the ordinaries themselves, or of those delegated by them, or by any other means eluding the judgment of the ecclesiastical court, have recourse to chanceries or other secular courts, and procure thence prohibitions and even penal mandates to be decreed against the said ordinaries and delegates and executed against them ; also those who make and execute these decrees, or who give aid, counsel, countenance or favour to them."

" Sect. 19. Further, we excommunicate and anathematize all and every magistrates and judges, notaries, scribes, executors, sub-executors, any ways intruding themselves in capital or criminal causes against ecclesiastical persons by processing, banishing, or apprehending them, or pronouncing or executing any sentences against them, without the special, particular and express license of this holy apostolical See ; also those who extend such licences to persons or cases not expressed, or any other way unjustly abuse them ; although the offenders should be counsellors, senators, presidents, chancellors, vice-chancellors, or intitled by any other name."

" Sect. 22. In fine, none may be absolved from the aforesaid censures by any other than by the pope of *Rome*, unless he be at the point of death, nor even then, unless he giveth caution to stand to the commands of the church, and give satisfaction"————

" Sect. 30. Let no man therefore infringe, or boldly and rashly oppose this our letter of excommunication, anathematization,

infallible: it is impoffible for infallibility to err; and, therefore, whilft Popery has any exiftence, it

tization, interdict, innovation, innodation, declaration, proteftation, abolition, revocation, commiffion, command and pleafure : but if any one fhall prefume to attempt it ; let him know that he fhall incur the difpleafure of Almighty God, and of his bleffed apoftles *Peter* and *Paul*."

Given at *Rome* from St. *Peter*, in the year of our Lord's incarnation, 1610, the 8th of *April*, in the fifth year of our popedom.

James Brambilla. *Mag. Curf.*

In the Year 1765.

A genuine copy of a Popifh excommunication, found amongft the papers of *Philip Dunn*, deceas'd, a Popifh bifhop, at his houfe in the county of *Wicklow*, pronounced by him againft *Francis Freeman*, one of his parifhioners, who at that time embraced the Proteftant religion. Faithfully tranflated from the Latin original, by Dr. *Tooker*.

" By authority of God the Father Almighty, and the bleffed virgin *Mary*, and of St. *Peter* and St. *Paul*, and all the holy faints, We excommunicate *Francis Freeman*, late of the county of *Dublin*, but now of *Juck-mill*, in the county of *Wicklow*, that in fpite of God and St. *Peter*, and in fpite of all the holy faints, and in fpite of our moft holy father the pope, (God's vicar on earth) and in fpite of our right reverend father in God, *Philip Dunn*, our diocefan, and worfhipful canons, who ferve God daily : hath apoftatized to a moft damnable religion, full of herefy and blafphemy ; excommunicated let him be, and delivered over to the devil, as a perpetual malefactor, and fchifmatick, accurfed let him be in all cities, and in all towns, in fields, in ways, in yards, in houfes, and in all other places,

It *muſt neceſſarily* be in future, what it hath been in times paſt.

Perhaps we may be told, that Popery is not tolerated : but where ſhall we draw the line between Toleration, and a repeal of every legal reſtriction; a removal of every diſcouragement to the growth of Popery?

In the preceding ſection, we have endeavoured to demonſtrate, that, by the late Act, all the laws againſt Popery are virtually, and the moſt eſſential, actually repealed; and, that the Pa-

places, whether lying or riſing, walking or running, leaning or ſtanding, waking or ſleeping, eating or drinking, or whatſoever thing he does : beſides we ſeparate him from the threſhold and all good prayers of the church ; from the participation of the holy Jeſus; from all ſacraments, chapels, and altars; from the holy bread and holy water, from all the merit of God's holy prieſts and religious men, and from their cloyſters and all pardons, privileges, grants and immunities, which all the holy popes have granted them ; and we give him over utterly to the fiend ; and let him quench his ſoul when dead in the pains of hell-fire, as this candle is quenched and put out. And let us pray to God, our lady, St. *Peter* and St. *Paul,* that all the ſenſes of his body may fail as now the light of this candle is gone ; except he come on ſight hereof, and openly confeſs his damnable hereſy and blaſphemy, and by repentance make amends as much as in him lies to God, our lady, St. *Peter,* and the worſhipful company of this church ; and as the ſtaff of this holy croſs now falls down, ſo may he, except he recants and repents."

Signed " Philip Dunn."

piſts

pifts conftrue it as a virtual repeal of all the Penal ftatutes, is evidenced by their prefent conduct. They are building, purchafing, and hiring buildings for mafs houfes: they are fetting up fchools and feminaries of learning, in different parts of this metropolis and kingdom. They prefume on the lenity of government; and ufe various artifices to enfnare the children of the poor, and to pervert the ignorant to their deftructive errors: they even infult Proteftant minifters in the difcharge of their duty.

Did they not underftand that the laws againft buying and felling Popifh books were repealed, they would not have dared to publifh an abftract of the *Douay Catechifm:* formerly they were cautious, even in bringing books into the realm, though printed abroad; or if they ventured to print, yet never to put the place where they were printed, or advertife them for fale; but circulated them, in a private manner: whereas, fince the paffing of the late Act of Parliament, they advertife their books and pamphlets in the public papers; and the publifher of the abftract of the *Douay Catechifm,* printed in 1779, has not only put his name and place of abode on the title page; but has told us, in capitals, that it is WITH PERMISSION.

Let us now attend to the fatal confequences that will probably refult from this repealing ftatute; and they appear truly alarming. The chief difcouragements to Popery are removed, and the Proteftant child of a Papift is now in no better a fituation, than his Popifh progeny. Jefuits and Popifh priefts will now take encouragement to refort hither, and compafs fea and land, to make profelytes: and Popifh teachers will be equally affiduous in feducing the children of the poor. Books will be publifhed, catechifms difperfed, and no pains fpared to captivate the unwary.

But let us look forward to pofterity, and the confequences appear yet more fatal. *Policy will teach the Papifts to be cautious at prefent, left they fhould alarm the Legiflature.* They are, therefore, now working by their emiffaries, in a fecret manner; but the evils will be feen and felt hereafter.

By educating our children, they are fapping and undermining the very foundation of our conftitution, in church and ftate. The Papifts, reftrained from purchafing, have, for many years, been accumulating money: they may now expend it to advantage. It is a melancholy confideration, that lands are not worth, at this time, fo much as they were, by feveral years purchafe. This is owing to the fcarcity of fpecie; but there is not fuch a fcarcity with the Papifts. The neceffity of the times will compel many to part with their

their eftates; and Papifts have an opportunity of purchafing for lefs than their value, and thereby of getting great part of the landed property of the kingdom into their own hands. Being enabled to purchafe, and capacitated to inherit, they will acquire an increafe of power, as their landed property increafes; and, by their landed property, will certainly, in a future period, *influence our elections in Parliament.*

By an influence in parliamentary elections, a future Parliament may be found endued with fuch a liberal fpirit of Toleration, as to remove the Teft Act; to qualify them for offices of magiftracy, and give them an opportunity of fitting in both Houfes of Parliament; or Papifts (as they can have difpenfations for oaths) may think it a duty they owe to the church of Rome, and by jefuitical fophiftry be taught, that it is no fin to put on the profeffion of Proteftantifm * for a

feafon

* That his holinefs of Rome authorifes fuch conduct, is evident from the cafe of *Parfons.* This *jefuit* was appointed fuperior in a miffion to England, in order to promote Popery in this kingdom. But he and his colleagues could not fafely come into thefe realms, becaufe *Pius* V. had not only abfolved the fubjects of queen *Elizabeth* from their oath of allegiance, but pronounced an *anathema* againft all thofe who fhould obey her. However, *Gregory* XIII. removed this hinderance, for he gave them a faculty, difpenfing with their obedience to the queen, notwithftanding the bull of his pre-

E   deceffor

feafon, to obtain feats in Parliament, that they may ferve the interefts of Popery.

Should fuch a period arrive, and unlefs wife and timely meafures are taken to prevent it, moft affuredly it will, where then will be the fafety of the Proteftant fucceffion in the illuftrious houfe of Hanover? and what fecurity will our pofterity have for the prefervation of their civil and religious liberties?

Nor are thefe fatal events improbable; perhaps not very remote!—If Papifts have power, it muft be ufed to fpread and exalt Popery throughout the land: and fhould fuch a period arrive, Papifts will then once more have the fword of magiftracy in their hands; England will again be deluged with the blood of martyrs, our liberties be exchanged for bondage; and the Proteftant religion be removed, to make room for Popifh fuperftition.

The laft obfervation that we fhall make on the confequences refulting from the late Act, feems to us of the utmoft importance, and demands the moft ferious attention.

In that Act of Parliament, the oaths of Allegiance and Supremacy, and the oath of Abjuration, are comprehended in one form; and, to ac-

deceffor. Thus Papifts of the worft fort appeared Proteftant fubjects, and this by papal authority.

Biograph. Diction. Life of Parfons.

3

commodate

commodate the Papifts, as was mentioned in the preceding fection, the words, " *ecclefiaftical* or " *fpiritual*," are omitted, and the words, " *tempo-* " *ral* or *civil*," inferted in their ftead. No Papift could confcientioufly have fworn, that the pope and bifhops appointed by him, had no *ecclefiaf- tical* or *fpiritual* authority or pre-eminence; when every Papift, as fuch, neceffarily owes implicit obedience, in fpiritual matters, to the pope of Rome. The words *ecclefiaftical* or *fpiritual*, are, therefore, omitted ; and the words *temporal* or *civil*, fubftituted ; and, by this very material alteration in the form of the oath, the *fpiritual* and *ecclefiaftical* jurifdiction of the pope and Po- pifh prelates (for there are titular bifhops already appointed over every fee throughout the king- dom) is tacitly acknowledged, and virtually re- cognized, by the Legiflature.

But, by the acknowledgment of this foreign jurifdiction within thefe realms, the *king's Supre- macy, in fpiritual matters*, is given up, at leaft in part, to the bifhop of Rome ; by which means the conftitution is violated, and perjury is im- pofed on every Proteftant, who, to qualify him- felf for any office in church or ftate, is neceffi- tated to take the oath of Supremacy appointed . by the ftat. of Geo. I. and which every Proteftant to whom it is tendered, is bound to take at his peril. Alarming confideration indeed !

By this, every Proteftant is required on his oath to declare, " That no foreign prince, Perfon, prelate, ftate, or potentate hath, or ought to have, any jurifdiction, power, fuperiority, pre-eminence, or authority, *ecclefiaftical* or *fpiritual*, within thefe realms ;" though he knows that the pope, a foreign prince, and the prelates appointed by him, claim ecclefiaftical and fpiritual jurifdiction, power, fuperiority, pre-eminence, and authority; and that the fame is now publicly recognized by an Act of the Legiflature : and that the laft oath of Supremacy, appointed to be taken by the Papifts, is framed in conformity thereto.

Some indeed may object, Did not the pope heretofore claim this jurifdiction, and Papifts acknowledge it; and were not Proteftants under the fame difficulty formerly, with refpect to the oath of fupremacy, as they are now? Certainly not : the pope might then command, and Papifts obey; but neither the one nor the other eftablifhed his *fpiritual* jurifdiction, whilft the laws refufed to admit it; and declared on the very face of the oath, that no foreign prince or prelate *hath, or ought to have,* any fuch authority within thefe realms.

But now, whilft the *temporal* and *civil jurifdiction* of the pope is excluded, his *ecclefiaftical* and *fpiritual authority* is, by omitting the words, *ecclefiaftical* and *fpiritual,* in the form of the oath, tacitly affented to: nor will a confcientious Proteftant teſtant be ſatisfied with being told, that he may ſafely take the oath of ſupremacy, notwithſtanding the alteration in the Popiſh oath; as he knows that no foreign ſtate, potentate, or prelate, *ought to have* any juriſdiction within theſe realms: he is to ſwear that they *have not*, as well as that *they ought not* to have any ſuch authority: which, before the recognition thereof by the late Act of Parliament, he might do, without wounding his conſcience.

It is in vain to tell us, that the pope *ought to have* no power, we ſee it is *now* acknowledged that he *hath*; and, therefore, can never take the oath of Supremacy, without involving ourſelves in the guilt of perjury: unleſs the laws, in that reſpect, are put on their former footing.

Are theſe the conſequences of this Act; and ſhall we be indifferent? Have we no regard for our welfare, and for the deareſt intereſts of poſterity? Shall we perjure and ruin ourſelves without making one generous effort?—Heaven forbid! Let us be rouſed to a conſideration of our ſtate: let us apply to government to obtain redreſs. We have reaſon to hope they would attend to our application, and remedy the evils apprehended from that improvident Act. But if they refuſe, we ſhall have nothing to reproach ourſelves with: we ſhall have diſcharged our duty; and, armed with conſcious integrity, be prepared for every event.

C O N.

CONCLUSION.

The absolute necessity of an application to Parliament for redress; and the constitutional mode of obtaining it.

UPON a review of the foregoing observations on the tendency and operation of the late Act of Parliament, is it not evident, that it is tantamount to a Toleration of Popery; a virtual repeal, and an actual suspension, of all the Penal laws against the Papists; and that it will be productive of the most fatal consequences?

The present state of Popery is truly alarming, and calls for immediate and spirited exertions, to prevent its further progress in this nation. To be indifferent or silent, at such a crisis, when all that is dear to us as men and christians, is at stake; would be ungrateful to the memory of our ancestors, injurious to ourselves, and unjust to generations yet unborn.

Though it be the desire of every true friend to civil and religious liberty, that Toleration should be built on the broadest basis; yet, to tolerate Popery, is to encourage what by Toleration itself we mean to destroy, a spirit of persecution and bigotry of the most notorious kind.

Papists

Papifts own a foreign head as fupreme, who can difpenfe with the *moft facred oaths* : and, therefore, no confidence can be put in their moft folemn proteftations. They have filled our land with blood, and alarmed us with maffacres, rebellion, and treafon : and fhall we, out of love to Popery, endanger· the peace of government and the fafety of the ftate? What meritorious actions of the Papifts entitle them to fuch favour at our hands.

The people of Great Britain have lately had ftriking proofs of the *fincerity of Popifh affurances*, from the *infidious conduct* of our *Roman Catholic neighbours*. FRANCE not only publicly protefted againft the conduct of our American colonies, but proceeded fo far in her *plan of duplicity*, as to order the *American privateers ·to leave her ports*; and SPAIN gave us to underftand, that fhe was too much interefted for her own colonies, to encourage fuch an example of difobedience to the mother country.

Our Miniftry, fatisfied with thefe *delufive affurances*, trufted to the *amity* of France and Spain, and refted in fecurity : they knew that TREACHERY was no part of the fyftem of BRITISH POLITICS ; and expected *that fincerity* from the houfe of Bourbon, which characterifes our conduct, and which is the glory of this nation.

What

What was the confequence? at the very time when Papifts were receiving favours from this government, our *profeffing friends* laid afide the mafque, and appeared in the blackeft colours of *bafenefs* and *perfidy*. Forgetting their public difavowals of the American caufe, and their folemn proteftations to the Britifh miniftry; their *moft Chriftian and Catholic majefties*, without the leaft provocation, contrary to the faith of treaties, and to the law of nations, united for our deftruction.

And fhall we, after fuch infidious conduct from Roman Catholic nations, truft to the *temporifing affurances* of Papifts, and put weapons into their hands, to be turned againft ourfelves?—Is this a time to look to them for fupport?—Rather, let us unite for the defence of our country, and the Proteftant in'ereft, againft all foreign and internal enemies: let us, as a nation, acknowledge God, and depend upon his Providence for fuccefs: and we need not fear the united efforts of our *perjured* and *inveterate* foes.

Having pointed out the fatal confequences of the late Act of Parliament; to remedy the evils, let the Proteftants, throughout the kingdom, affociate as one man, and apply to government for redrefs: and thus fhew, that the fenfe of the people at large is not to favour Popery: and that,

that, whilft they are fupported by *Britiſh Proteſ-tants*, they have nothing to fear from *Popiſh ad-verſaries*.

Something is neceſſary to be done, to aſſure the nation in general, and Papiſts in particular, that it is not the intention of the Legiſlature, to encourage the growth of Popery. Papiſts are infolent and prefuming: and nothing but a law to repeal or qualify the late Act, can keep them within the bounds of allegiance and decency.

Such an Act is abfolutely neceſſary to fatisfy the minds of all true Proteſtants; to relieve us from the impoſition of perjury, occafioned by the late alteration of the oath of fupremacy in favour of the Papiſts; to fave the conſtitution from being violated; to preferve the Proteſtant intereſt in this kingdom from that imminent danger, with which it is threatened; and to fecure the Proteſtant fucceſſion in the family of His prefent Majeſty.

Our conſtitution hath marked out the mode of obtaining redrefs; and declares, that it is the right of the fubject to petition. Let petitions be circulated throughout the kingdom: let the clergy of the eſtabliſhment and Proteſtant miniſters of every denomination, and all who are zealous for the welfare and fafety of the Proteſtant religion, cordially unite, and ſtrenuouſly exert themſelves on this important occaſion.

Let

Let petitions againſt the Popiſh Bill be ſent to Parliament, with numerous ſignatures from every county, city, and corporation ; and from other reſpectable bodies of people. Let our repreſentatives be inſtructed by their conſtituents, to ſupport theſe petitions in the houſe ; and, as the eve of a general election is approaching, we have reaſon to hope, that theſe inſtructions will be attended to. Should they be neglected, we ſoon ſhall have an opportunity in our hands, of electing members more attentive to the voice of the people, and the preſervation of the Proteſtant intereſt.

If ſuch meaſures be adopted by Proteſtants with unanimity, and proſecuted with ſpirit, government may then with ſafety relieve us from our fears, by repealing the late Act ; and have nothing to dread from the reſentment of the Papiſts.

But, ſhould it be objected, that, as the Act is paſſed, it would now be dangerous to repeal it : let us at leaſt apply for a reſtraining Act, to qualify, amend, and explain the Popiſh bill.

An Act, to declare, that the former Penal Statutes are in full force, and that perſons ſhall be duly encouraged in putting them into execution, to prevent the further growth of Popery.

An Act, to amend the form of the oath in that paſſed for the relief of the Papiſts, that Proteſtants, ftants, who are required to take the oath of Supremacy, may not be neceffitated to incur the guilt of wilful perjury.

An Act, to prevent the Papifts (if they muft be permitted to acquire landed property) from interefting themfelves, directly or indirectly, in any election for members of Parliament, on pain of forfeiture of their eftates.

An Act, to prevent jefuits from reforting hither under heavy penalties, and to prohibit the attempts of Papifts to pervert Proteftants to their erroneous tenets, on pain of exemplary punifhment.

And laftly, (if Papifts muft be permitted to teach thofe of their own principles in private) an Act, to reftrain them from keeping public fchools, and teaching the children of Proteftant parents, on pain of perpetual imprifonment or banifhment.

As to declaring the former laws againft the Papifts yet in force; if the late Act were defigned only to repeal detached parts of a fingle ftatute, and the former laws are not underftood to be affected thereby; it will be an Act of kindnefs to the Papifts, to put them on their guard, by fuch a declaration; or, otherwife, their zeal to profelyte may expofe them to difagreeable confequences.

It is not meant that thefe ftatutes fhould be

executed

executed with feverity. Whilft Papifts conti-
nue peaceable, and do not attempt to diffufe
their pernicious principles, what will they have
to apprehend from that fpirit of lenity, with
which thefe ftatutes have ever been enforced?

We prefume that it would be better if the
late Act of Parliament were totally repealed, and
the laws againft the Papifts placed upon their
former footing. But if that cannot be obtained,
a qualifying Act, with fome fuch reftrictions as
thofe abovementioned, feems abfolutely neceffary. Thus the Papifts would be curbed, but
not crufhed ; they would not be perfecuted, nor
could they perfecute ; the *grand objects* of this
ASSOCIATION would be obtained ; the Proteftant religion would be preferved ; the Britifh
conftitution fecured ; and the Hanoverian fucceffion eftablifhed upon the firmeft bafis.

FINIS.